Sherri Waas Shunfenthal's *Sacred Voices: Women of Genesis Speak* is one woman's open hearted exploration of Biblical women's lives from their perspective. For Sherri, these women are understood as neighbors, sisters and friends. Her approach has the dual effect of making these legendary women accessible, while simultaneously elevating all women's lives to the mythic realm.

-Sandra Kammann: Anthropologist, Director and Performing Artist

Sacred Voices is a deceptive collection of poems. The simple and delicate language does not prepare the reader for the powerful insights into the women of Genesis. I would not go so far as to say that only a woman could write these poems, but a woman did, and the nuances, the subtle moods, thoughts and feelings explored in this work enrich Genesis. When Sarah, for instance, well past the age of child bearing, laughs at the news that she will have a son within the year, the patriarchal original has her deny her laughter as so many women have had to deny their inner selves for centuries. Sherri Waas Shunfenthal, with the wisdom born of her own motherhood, understands the complexity of Sarah's laugh -- disbelief, fear, regret, and most importantly, simple joy -- the laugh of a woman fulfilled. In so many ways, these poems set the record straight.

-Donald R, Gallehr
Director, Northern Virginia Writing Project
George Mason University

To the plethora of recent female midrash, Sherri Waas Shunfenthal adds a telling of the Bible tales in a fresh, naive voice as though the tales were being re-read for the first time. This works best, of course, where the story really is fresh. Shunfenthal is at her best creating here-to-fore nameless characters such as the wives of Lot and of Noah where she can paint with a clean brush, without regard to earlier models.

-Henny Wenkart, Editor
Jewish Women's Literary Annual

i

Sherri Waas Shunfenthal has given new meaning to some of the ancient Biblical characters. Her midrashic poetry challenges us to try to understand what our ancient heroines were thinking and experiencing. Sherri's poems are deeply spiritual, causing us to think about the meaning of our lives in relationship to our Biblical heroines.

-Rabbi Bruce Aft
Congregation Adat Reyim in Springfield, Virginia

Sherri Waas Shunfenthal's poetry on the women of Genesis sent me scurrying back to the scripture to reread the Biblical stories again. Indeed, Sherri's poems *are* the stories - fresh and new! She is truly an artist of words painting the long narratives into pictures of great feelings. I could feel the power of Eve, Sarah's silent laughter, and the agony of Rachel's lost love. These Biblical women speak out of centuries long past the timelessness of feminine love and longing, of perseverance, jealousy, and hope.

Ms. Shunfenthal's creativity and intent are summed up at the end of her poem "Dinah Speaks":

Hear her story
Do not let her vanish
Into history.

-The Rev. Dr. Beth P. Braxton
Burke Presbyterian Church
Virginia

Dedication

Sherri Waas Shunfenthal writes:
This book is dedicated to the women who have inspired me: in memory of my grandmothers, Clara Wasserman and Alice Waas and Aunt Mary; in appreciation and admiration of my mother, Sylvia Waas, my Aunts: Natalie, Annie, Celia and Betty, "sister" Betsy , cousin Sharon, Sylvia Shunfenthal and my daughter, Jennifer.

Judybeth Greene writes:
To my mom and my Aunt Joyce and Aunt Lois, who brought a spark to our Passover seders by changing all references to God in the Passover readings to the feminine.

Sacred Voices:
Women of Genesis Speak

Sherri Waas Shunfenthal
Illustrations Judybeth Greene
Editor J. Thomas Hetrick

Pocol Press

POCOL PRESS

Published in the United States of America
by Pocol Press.
6023 Pocol Drive
Clifton, Virginia 20124
http://members.xoom.com/Vonderahe/pocolpress.htm

Publisher's Cataloguing-in-Publication

Shunfenthal, Sherri Waas.
    Sacred voices : women of Genesis speak / Sherri
    Waas Shunfenthal ; illustrations Judybeth Greene ;
    editor J. Thomas Hetrick. – 1st ed.
    p. cm.
    Includes bibliographical references.
    LCCN: 99-
    ISBN: 1-929763-07-7

    1. Women in the Bible—Poetry.   I. Greene,
Judybeth.   II. Title.

PS3569.H797S23 2000   811'.6
                        QBI99-1969

Cover art: "Eve hands down the apple"
Rear Cover Art: "Sarah laughing"
    by Judybeth Greene, © 2000.

Acknowledgements

Sherri Waas Shunfenthal wishes to especially thank Rabbi Bruce Aft for his time, encouragement and delightful dialogue about women of Torah; members of Parsha study group special friends Hazel and Ray Solomon, Linda Braverman, and Amy Leibowitz for insight into Torah topics; all my friends at Adat Reyim who listen to my poetry and lend support and so many other wonderful people; Jim Charlton, former High School English teacher who kept me from being a closet poet; my parents who inspired a love of words; my brother, who is a first class investigative reporter; husband Mike and kids for giving me the write time and their unfailing love; J. Thomas Hetrick and Judybeth Greene for helping to make a dream a reality.

Judybeth Greene writes: Collaborative work between a poet and an artist has a special energy, involving a respect for one another's process and deeper insight into the nature of the work. I wish to thank Sherri Waas Shunfenthal first and foremost for allowing me this special opportunity.

I wish to thank the members of Fabrangen, a havurah (community) in Washington D.C. that exemplifies the best of the Jewish renewal movement, for sharing their hearts and minds and expanding my judaic knowledge and giving me a spiritual home. My art lives in large part due to the influence of this community.

Special thanks go to Deborah Kant, Lloyd Wolf, Paula Wolfsson, Janice Steinschneider, Margie Jones, Deborah Kolodny, Melissa Crowe, Eric Rosenthal, Lori Hymon, and Susan Fribush for supporting my creativity and continuing Jewish exploration. Special thanks also go to Penny Barringer at Discover Graphics for teaching me the art of color monotypes, Pepe Coronado at the Corcoran School of Art for teaching me to manipulate my work on the computer, and to Ruth Cahnmann, Vincent Baines, Jane Singlay, Tricia Tingle, Richard Dellheim, Chris Herren and Tom Rall for their encouragement of my artistic and creative endeavors. I also must thank the person who seems to be at my side more than not, my man Ron Fagnani, for his consistency, love and support. Also special thanks go to my colleagues at work: Joe Rich, Becky Wertz, Zita Johnson-Betts, Donna Murphy, Elizabeth Johnson, Barry Weinberg, Anita Hodgkiss and Bill Lann Lee for understanding, appreciating, and accommodating my connection with my art. I also wish to thank Doris Kafka for her help in making my dreams and goals a reality.

My love and forever thanks go, of course, to my parents, Roberta Greene Sacks and Alan Greene, and my siblings Debbie and David Greene for growing up as part of their world.

Table of Contents

Introduction

Several years ago, I joined a Parsha study group (Bible study). Parsha means "portion" in Hebrew so we examined a portion of the Torah (the scrolls of the Bible) that corresponded with that week's reading at synagogue. Together with our Rabbi, our Parsha study group questioned, debated and explored the text of the Torah. Our discussions were lively. Genesis inspired the most exciting interchanges because the stories of Genesis are filled with love, longing, passion, jealousy and betrayal. (The first soap opera ever written.)

The Biblical stories of the Torah are written in narrative form. Narratives tend to tell primarily of events or actions. We learn in detail the motivations, thoughts, feelings, and actions of men such as Abraham, Isaac, Joseph, or Jacob. However, we see the women's lives in fragments, often only in relation to the men's lives. Many times, the actions of the women are given a negative interpretation.

My Parsha study group left me longing to know more about these women. What were their motivations, thoughts, and feelings? What clues exist in the Biblical texts that give us more insight into their stories? Can there be other interpretations about their lives that we don't know because details were erased by the patriarchal society of the time? The Biblical stories of the Torah have lived with us for over 5, 000 years. We can continue to make new discoveries about the text. As we make these discoveries, we find that the stories have relevance to our own lives. Stories have power to awaken us and give us insight.

There is a lot of word play in the Torah and many ways that one word can be interpreted. For example, we spent one Parsha study group debating the relevance of the word "settled." The Torah says that Jacob "settled" in the land of his father. We asked numerous questions such as, "Why did he 'settle' later in his life?" "Do we have more of a tendency to desire settling down when we are older?" "Does 'settling' imply a feeling of contentment that Jacob did not have earlier in his life?" "Does 'settling in the land of his father' mean that

Jacob acknowledged his roots and now had a sense of belonging?"
"Did it mean he finally stopped running from ghosts of his past?"
"What makes us feel 'settled' in our own lives?"

Poetry and Bible stories

Poetry delves into the mystery of what is common and known to bring it to our attention and present it in a new light. I hope I have breathed life into the souls of the Biblical women and given new understanding to their stories.

I am not a Biblical scholar or historian. Poetry is a personal interpretation. However, every time I read the Biblical stories, they seem vibrant and alive. There is new meaning and depth to be found in each reading. As Karen Armstrong says in her book, *In the Beginning*, "...Genesis has been treasured not for the light it throws on the irretrievably distant past but for its timeless relevance to the present."

Often, my poetry evolved from questions. For instance, why does Rebekah appeal to God to understand why her pregnancy was so difficult? I identified with Rebekah's discomfort at bearing the weight of twins, as I was also pregnant with twins. They both had very different personalities in the womb. One moved constantly, giving me heartburn, while the other scared me at times by being still. Sometimes, they seemed to wrestle and bump into each other. There were many sleepless nights. I put myself in Rebekah's place and could understand her calling to God.

Genesis, to me, is the most exciting book of the Torah because it about our desire- to discover ourselves, our relationship to God and our destinies. The women and men in Genesis are passionate, full of life, and they exhibit strong emotions. They are not perfect and there is much to learn from them. The Torah provides glimpses into their relationships, mistakes, achievements, and their legacies from one generation to the next.

Let us view the Bible stories to see who we were, who we are now, and who we want to be in the future. We need to blow life into the soul of these stories. We need to create our own Midrash so that when the next century dawns, men and women work together, share our stories, and find meaning in them.

Midrash

In Judaism, we have Midrash -- interpretive teachings that attempt to fill in details left untold. Midrash, like poetry, explores many layers. Similar to archeology, Midrash digs deeper for meaning. Ancient Rabbis originally created Midrash so the text would be more accessible to the people. Unfortunately, many Midrashic texts were interpretations by men in a patriarchal society. The women's stories were left silent or looked upon in an unfavorable light.

Midrash attempts to fill in gaps. In many ways, the Torah seems like a puzzle with major events recorded but details left unsaid. Why did Lot's wife look back after having been warned not to? What would you have done?

I created Midrash in writing some of these poems. Inside are stories I created gleaned from the information I learned from the texts, discussions, and other Midrashic sources. We are forever part of the continuing history of our world. Let us hear the women. By entering their world and viewing their flaws, strengths and triumphs, we begin to rediscover ourselves.

Evolving Together

If men and women weave their stories together, and if we see how important we were to each other's past, and not see our stories as separate, we can better see our future together, men and women working together in the 21st century. Let us hear each other's voices, let us listen. Let us feel lucky that we have choices and guard our choices carefully. Let us keep evolving together.

The women's stories in this book are in the order in which they appear in Genesis. At the end of this book is commentary containing the location of the women's stories in Genesis, and some thoughts about each woman.

-Sherri Waas Shunfenthal

ARTIST'S STATEMENT

I first met Sherri Waas Shunfenthal through her poetry when I listened to her read one of her meditative poems at a candle light havdalah service at the D.C. Jewish Community Center. I was so moved that immediately after the service, I asked her if I could use her poetry in my artwork. Little did I know that she was looking for an artist to illustrate her work. That was the beginning of our collaborative work together as well as the beginning of a creative and nurturing friendship. It has been a privilege and an honor to be in her presence.

Now a word about how these specific images came to be. The pictures featured in this book were specifically created to accompany Sherri's lyrical poetry. These images were created through a form of printmaking called "monotypes." This process is known by artists for the painterly quality of the resulting work. For these works, I started with a blank metal sheet on which I rolled purple, turquoise or black inks. Then I drew images in the ink by using a Q-tip or the back of a brush to withdraw the ink and create white lines. In some pieces, I then used a brush to paint other areas with different color inks. At times, I also used turpentine to allow the ink to spread into muted patterns. When I was done working on these images, I placed paper over the inked metal and ran them each through a hand-operated press. The pressure of the press embossed the paper and transferred the ink to the paper for a one-of-a-kind print. Although many of the images are published here in black and white, the quality of the line and spirit will hopefully transcend the color barrier.

-Judybeth Greene

Lilith

The Night Sky Belongs to Lilith

"Male and female, God created them and blessed them."
(Genesis 1:27)

Lilith
was just awakening
longing for herself
when she left Adam
being born in that beginning.

Lilith
chose to fly away from Adam
to the Red Sea, symbol of freedom
a place of promise.

Lilith
now moves freely over many lands
celebrates herself
knows her own powers. She gathers
stars for the night sky.

Lilith
lights the darkness. The stars
are her offspring. She calls
each one by name.

Lilith
is no demon nor is she haunted.
She travels in darkness and shadow
waiting for the dawn
waiting for women to waken
have no fear.

Lilith
has been waiting 5,000 years
whispering in the night, "Awaken
to powers and possibilities. See the
freedom of each twinkling star
dancing in the dark. Reach for stars."
Wholeness comes in darkness
and illumination.

Eve and the Apple

"So when the woman saw that the tree was good for food, and that it was a delight to the eyes, and that the tree was desired to make one wise, she took of its fruit and ate." (Genesis 3:6)

Season of change
red-gold-orange-yellow-green
leaves burn brightly on branches.
Apples hang as if they are prizes
for the beauty of the Fall.

Eve is awakened by the brightness.
She notices a round red glistening
apple covered by shinysmooth skin
of polished brilliance like the sun.

She feels a yearning, an unexplained
hunger. The snake coaxes, "Reach,
reach, reach, don't be afraid.
All knowledge lies here,"
and before understanding
she reaches upward. Palm and fingers
encircle the lustrous, silky dream
of her desire. She feels the smooth
round fullness of it as she moves
the apple toward her mouth.

Her teeth crunch crisp ripeness.
She tastes the soursweet
juice and pulp rolling
about her tongue.
Each bite an awareness
of a world about to begin.

She hungers.
Awe fills her-
a sense of responsibility
to satisfy
this hunger
that is oh so sweet.

Adam & his remote

Eve Finds Adam after Tasting the Apple

(This prose poem was written after reading Mark Twain's *Diary of Adam and Eve*. I tried to incorporate Twain's delightful tongue-in-cheek style into the poem.)

Eve goes in search of Adam after tasting the apple. She feels filled with a sense of wonder and enchantment. She hopes Adam is not busy with the new toy he devised which he calls a remote. He uses it to watch the sunrise and sunset over and over again. Sun up, sun down, sun up, sun down. Eve does not know how that can be very interesting.

She enjoys interacting with the animals. This very morning she helped a bird build its nest. They had chattered amiably about the other birds, the weather and which trees are best to build in. Later she enjoyed having a cat curl up in her lap. Then she spoke with the serpent who enticed her to try the delicious fruit on the most beautiful tree in the garden.

The tree had no name. Eve would have to think of a name although Adam did not like for Eve to name things. "That's my job," he would declare in a big voice. His name for things seemed so silly sometimes. Her names had meaning. "I will call the lovely tree A Pull tree," she thought, "because I had to reach to pull the fruit down." She was eager to tell Adam all about it.

Adam saw Eve walking toward him. There was something changed about her. Her cheeks glowed. She looked brighter. "Eve, you look so...." He stammered trying to find words. Finding words was not easy for Adam.

"I have a surprise for you, Adam," she said as she drew the APull from behind her back. "Here," she offered. "Isn't this beautiful? It is for you."

Adam kept looking at Eve. He thought, "She is quite beautiful." He had never had this thought before. He reached for the gift. "Eat it like this," she said as she showed him. He tasted the fruit. It had an incredible taste that filled him.

7

Adam had been in a deep sleep at the beginning of time. He felt himself awakening again. He felt powerful, anxious, full of new thoughts, sudden insight. He was bursting with understanding. The remote dropped from his hand. Adam grabbed Eve's arm.

They went running through the garden. "Do you know why leaves change color, Eve?" He started explaining. Eve looked at Adam more closely. He was not as dull as she had thought. He was interesting. He wanted to interact with her. She was excited. She felt strong, powerful and full of new insights, too. They ran around the garden looking at things as if for the first time.

"The garden seems so different; doesn't it Eve?" Adam asked. Then ran from one area to the next shouting with joy and sharing new-found knowledge. They touched everything. They stopped to look at things in wonder. Everything seemed so exciting. Soon they were near the tree. "Let's sit under the APull tree and rest awhile, Adam," Eve said.

They sat. Adam was feeling something he had never felt before. He had the strangest urge. He put his lips against Eve's lips. Her cheeks got a deeper red color. He could not remember if her cheeks had ever done this before. It was very strange. Adam did not understand this. With all his new-found knowledge, he knew intuitively that he would probably never really understand her. He wanted to see if this would happen again. So he did the thing with his lips once more. She got all rosy again. "Your cheeks look like the APull," he told her. Then he started turning all rosy color. Eve suddenly felt as if her whole body was rosy. Without thinking she pulled some leaves in front of her to cover herself up. Adam quickly did the same.

Adam realized which tree they were under. "Eve, this is the Tree of Knowledge." "You are so smart, Adam," Eve sighed. "No, you don't understand, Eve, our lives are changed. God told me to stay away from this tree. We will have too much knowledge." She was so glad he said "we."

Off they ran together. With all their new found knowledge, they did not know that they could not hide from God, but they sure had a good time in the bushes until God found them.

Adam's Apple

Innocent and trustful
full of curiosity like a child,
Eve believed the serpent
when that serpent promised her
good things to come.

With that first full bite
of knowledge, she turned to see
Adam's serpent reaching
toward her. She put her
apple down. Adam took a bite.
They awoke inside each other.

Eve was Adam's apple when he finally
awoke. He knew there was no
turning back. "Flesh of my flesh,
bone of my bone, I will follow
you anywhere. You are my
temptation. My hunger
for you is great."

Adam trembled, "We may never
again feel safe." Eve
reassured him, "Together
we are safe."

Like the fruit of the tree
Eve and Adam ripened. God
admonished, "It is time to send
you from your home." And like
any good parent, God did not
intervene but watched over
them as they set upon a journey of
discovery.

They left their happy home
with heavy heart. No set
destination. Unexplored
beginnings stirring in their souls.

Eve

The serpent said to the woman, "...for God knows that when you eat of it your eyes will be opened, and you will be like God, knowing good and evil." (Genesis 3:5)

Eve
made us human
different from the other beasts.
Eve gave us insight,
curiosity and desire.
When Eve pulled that apple down,
it was a seed of wanting
to know, to blossom, to grow.

God looked down upon God's creation
and said "It is good. And since you dare,
woman, I will let only you know
about the true act of creation." And
God gave birth to Woman.

Woman pushes forth
pushes until life comes tumbling out.
Woman struggles with that push
but still thrusts Life forward.
Woman knows with all creation
comes some pain. Woman is Humble,
a Life-giver, Nurturer. Woman
looks upon all creatures
and says "There is good."

That first Birth Day is pure Eden-
Untouched, Naked, Beginning.

Men and women all come from Woman's
push out of the garden. Humans were just one
of many beasts before Eve ventured forth.

Man might try but
Woman cannot be tamed.
Woman will always reach...

Noah's Wife Speaks

"Noah was a righteous man, blameless in his generation. Noah walked
with God." (Genesis 6:9)

Noah, my man of the soil
walks with God.
He is a quiet man
faithful, dependable.
Up with the sun to plant,
he toils until nightfall.
Sometimes he drinks the fruit
of the vine to help him rest.

Noah is different from the wild
men of town. He is loyal, constant
like the sun and moon. Noah
senses weather patterns. Our fields
flourish. We are never hungry.

Noah listens. He hears God
tell him to build a house
that floats. Waters will come
cover the land. It is hard for me
to understand. Noah is told to build a
floating house, called an ark.

The ark must be
three hundred cubits in length
fifty cubits in width
three floors high.
Who has ever heard of a floating
house? Who has heard of a house
with three floors?

Noah builds. Our sons help
fell cypress trees for the wooden
ark. People from town come to watch.
They point their fingers. They steal wood.
Their laughter pierces like arrows

aimed at our hearts. "There are no
big rains," they chide. My boys hide
from their scorn.

I trust Noah. I must.
There is nowhere for a woman to go
alone with three sons. I stay,
watch, work the fields
trying to imagine a floating house.
I trust Noah. I must.

The Animals are our Friends

Noah is busy building.
My sons and I toil the soil
doing work that Noah once did.

We are isolated, alone.
My boys wander the forests
befriending wounded animals.
I bind the creatures' wounds with leaves,
cloth and mixtures of healing salts.
It comforts me to comfort the animals.

I learn their language in the same way
I understood my boys' shrieks and sighs
when they were babies. The animals
respond to me when I call.

A young fox follows me into the fields
each day as I work. He rubs his fur
against my legs. I laugh when
he darts away chasing squirrels.

My goose greets me mornings.
His haughty stance and low shrill squeal
scare the other animals so they do not
grab food as I feed them.

Rabbits pop out of holes
snatching food the others drop.
The brown long-eared rabbit
snuggles into my lap
while I grind meal for food.

My sons instinctively communicate
with the animals too. The animals
respond with long strings of singing
sound. The boys play tracking games
with them. The animals love
our lush fields and eat freely.

Three women wander the forests.
They also love the animals. They
will become the wives of my sons.

Together, we live happily under one roof-
my sons, their wives, the animals,
Noah and me. Noah's ark will be
large enough for us with all the
animals. We help build Noah's ark-
singing, sweating, shaping our future.

Time

"They went into the ark with Noah, two and two of all flesh in which there was the breath of life." (Genesis 7:15)

It is time to go
into the ark.
Every wild animal
every domestic animal
every creature that creeps
every creature that flies
male and female
two by two of every flesh
we gather.

It takes a week to summon
the animals to sanctuary.
We speak soothing sounds,
coaxing the animals into confinement.
They go reluctantly up the ramp
into the ark. The soft, comforting
voices of Shem, Ham and Japheth
calm them. Ham pulls hoofed
animals to be housed on the
second deck. Japheth tames large
beasts by steadfastly staring
into their bold eyes. He leads them
to the lowest deck. The rabbits, I bring
in my arms, the squirrels on my shoulders,
the dove is perched on my head.
My geese follow me into the ark.

Noah keeps an accounting of all who enter.
We are then sealed into safety.
One window overhead lets us watch
darkening clouds forming above us.
Heaven bursts open. Raging rains
pound the earth. Violence outside
shakes the ark making us shiver.
We are lifted into the air

as if we are clouds. The ark moves
onto the waters as floods fill the floors
and valleys of once dry land. Our ark tilts,
tosses. We tumble upon one another.
Stench of fear fills the ark.

We sway on giant swells of water.
We are like one large leaf
staying aloft in the midst of the rising ocean.
We move further, rising up on
raging waves then falling swiftly
but never going under.
Many of the animals get sick.
We are dizzy with fear.

It is several days before
the ark drifts onto calmer waters.
No more crashing waves. Noah keeps
track of days and night. Drowning rains
continue forty days and forty nights!

I cannot tell morning from evening.
There is so much work to do.
My sons, their wives and I clean the ark,
feed the animals, bind animals' wounds,
sing soothing songs, cook and care
for all of us. We are rocked gently
in the cradle of the ark. Waters
swirl around us slowly now.
We work, worry, wait.
Life on land is gone. Everything we
once knew is covered by water.
We are sheltered within the
safety of our ark.

Arc of Peace

Winds blow over the earth.
The waters spill away.
On the seventeenth day
of the seventeenth month our ark
comes to rest on Mount Ararat.

Noah sends out my dove.
She returns. Her feet could
not find dry land. Seven days later
Noah sends her out again. She returns with
an olive leaf in her beak. Life is sprouting
from the earth! The dove is anxious
to be free but Noah waits seven more days.
My dove does not return.
The earth is ready for us.

God directs Noah to come into the light.
Noah removes the cover of the ark.
Every wild animal
every domestic animal
every creeping creature
every flying creature
must be delivered
onto land now beginning to bloom.

The animals are unsteady.
Some are young. They do not remember
forests or fields. My beloved foxes,
horses, monkeys, cats,
rabbits, geese, birds,
I speak to each of them. They
nuzzle against me
afraid to travel from the familiar
dark comfort of the ark.

19

Wolves bark and bellow
wary of bright daylight.
Monkeys jump into my arms chattering
loudly while the wildcats
scamper away quickly into the woods.
Gently, my sons and I coax
each set of animals to descend
into sunlight. I cry as I say good-bye.
Noah keeps track of all who leave.
Japheth chases away the stragglers.
Order is restored unto life.

God's bow is set into the sky
forming an arc of bright
dazzling colors above us.
The animals walk through the arc
being born onto the land.

This world is ours.
Each time it rains, we see
the colorful arc of peace
between heaven and earth.
We remember.

We must protect the land.
Noah, my man of the soil
plants a vineyard.
We begin.

Messengers Come to Sarah's House

"... and lo, Sarah thy wife shall have a son." (Genesis 18:10)

Abraham sat resting in the heat
of the day. When he lifted his eyes
three men were in range
of his seeing. Abraham ran to them
offering to be their servant. He quickly
sought Sarah to make fine
meal cakes for the guests.

The mysterious strangers were hot,
hungry and weary. Their colorful clothes
did not seem dirty or dusty from traveling.
Sarah, curious, stayed within listening
range near the opening of the tent.

When Abraham joined the strangers,
they asked, "Where is Sarah, thy wife?"
Sarah, surprised to hear her name,
stood rooted like a tree listening.
One stranger told Abraham, "I will
return unto you this season next
year. Sarah shall have a son."

Sarah laughed heartily to herself.
She was old, beyond time
for bearing children. The stranger
asked, "Why did Sarah laugh?"
Sarah denied her laughter,
immediately fearful that these strangers
knew her inner self.

They knew her name
heard her silent laughter
came from distances unknown.
They must be messengers of God.
Hope filled Sarah
with a radiance that shone.
She shook with pure joy.
And Sarah laughed.

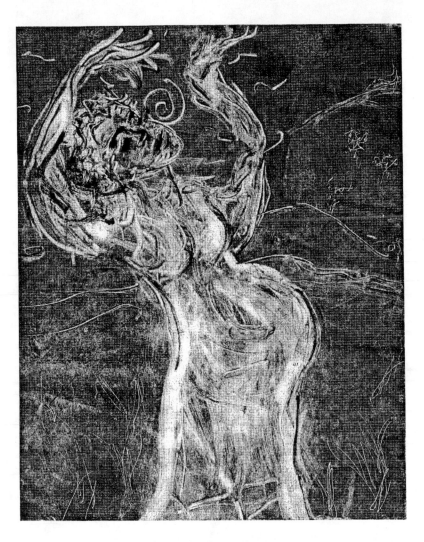

Sarah laughing

Sarah Laughed

"And Sarah laughed...." (Genesis 18:12)

And Sarah laughed
when the strangers came
to tell Abraham that she, Sarah
would bear a child of her own.

Sarah laughed
a laugh of disbelief
to think of bearing a child
now at her age.

And Sarah laughed
a nervous, fearful laugh
to think of carrying a child
late in life when her body
was not as supple
not as young, not as strong.

Sarah laughed
a regretful laugh
to think of rearing a child
when beauty, youth and energy
had begun to abate.

Then Sarah laughed.
Simply, joyfully
Sarah laughed. Aloud.

Sarah's Son

Sarah cherished Isaac
from the moment she felt him stir
inside her womb. Isaac was
her gift of laughter
sent from God
when hope had faded
like a distant dream.

Sarah struggled for many hours
before she gave birth to Isaac.
She panted, wept, cried out in pain
until Isaac showed his timid head.
He emerged silent but smiling.
Sarah laughed to see one so small
smiling.

Sarah brought him to her breast,
sang to him for hours. Isaac was slow
to suckle. Sarah swaddled
him in comfort, bound him to her.
She held him tightly in her
arms, wrapped him in her love.

Isaac was weaned late.
Sarah, older, was content to sit
with him. She was in no hurry.
Isaac grew slowly, knew
more of his mother's love
than a man's love.
Isaac's eyes were weak.
Sarah shared her vision with him.

Sarah's steady affection
taught Isaac patience. Isaac's trust
in God was simple and absolute
like his trust in his mother's love.

Isaac was not Ishmael.
Ishmael had a hunter's aggressiveness.
Ishmael sprang like a lion
at his enemies. Ishmael was mischievous,
sometimes cruel to Isaac
who usurped Abraham's attention.

Sarah sensed danger if Ishmael
stayed. Isaac was part of the
covenant with God.

Sarah must protect her son.

Hagar

An angel called to Hagar from heaven, saying, "What is wrong, Hagar?
Do not be afraid...Lift up your son in your arms, for I will make a great
nation of him." (Genesis 21:17)

Hagar
the handmaid
was the first known surrogate mother.
Neither wife nor constant companion
to Abraham, she bore his child
Ishmael.

Hagar loved the child.
Sarah loved the child
who was
and was not her own.

Hagar nursed and fed Ishmael.
Sarah sang Ishmael lullabies.
Abraham taught Ishmael
to be sharp with a bow
taught him what a boy needed
to know.

Ishmael needed to know
that he was loved.
He was loved.
He was first.
He was unrivaled
until Sarah bore Isaac
in her old age
when thoughts of bearing a child
had evaporated like a thousand dreams.

Sarah remembered God's promise.
Isaac, son of Abraham and Sarah
would inherit all that belonged to Abraham-
flocks, silver, land, and a great nation.

Hagar's son overshadowed the helpless
baby Isaac. Ishmael teased and taunted
him. Hagar was made to leave the home
she dared believe was her own.

Alone, with Ishmael, in the wilderness
Hagar cried out to God in anger,
in despair. She was without food
or hope. A well of water appeared.
She gave her son a drink. Hope
was restored. Hagar and Ishmael did not
starve in the wilderness. An angel spoke
promising to make Hagar's son
a great nation.

Ishmael fathered
the Arab nation.
Isaac fathered
the Hebrew nation.

Isaac and Ishmael,
half-brothers, together buried
their father, Abraham,
at the end of his days.

Sarah's Family Bound Together:
The Akedah

"When they came to the place that God had shown him, Abraham built an altar there and laid the wood. He bound his son Isaac and laid him on the altar, on top of the wood." (Genesis 22:9)

Abraham's Restlessness

Isaac was soft, innocent
and trusting. Sarah wrapped her love
around him like a protective shield.
Isaac was simple yet Sarah had faith.
Sarah remembered God's promise.

Abraham was growing older.
Did Abraham trust God's wisdom
in choosing this son as leader?
Abraham blamed Sarah for Isaac's
simplicity. Abraham thundered,
"He must become a man soon!"
Conflicted, Abraham wrestled with his
rage. "How can one so weak
be strong enough to lead?"

Softly like a sigh Abraham moaned,
"How will Isaac protect the fields,
make peace with our enemies?"
Sarah's man of action, Abraham
was close to weeping. Sarah's heart
was torn between the two men she loved.
She could not heal
words and wounds between them.

The Dream

Silently in his heart Abraham wished
that Isaac was more like Ishmael
strong and agile
ready with his bow
easily showing strength
able to plan for tomorrow.

Abraham had always been
a man of vision. He tried to see
a future with Isaac as leader
but he could not see. Abraham raged to God,
"Why did you give me a son of limited vision
who cannot see beyond this tent?"

Abraham tossed, moaned and mumbled
frequently in his sleep. This night
his face was bathed in sweat
though cool night air breezed through the tent.
Abraham's fist suddenly raised toward the night sky
then he punched the ground
once, twice, again and again calling
"Where are you?" Sarah heard and
answered, "Hineni." (I am here).
All went quiet.

In his dream a voice spoke
to Abraham. Was it God
who spoke? "You must sacrifice your son
for the sake of the future. Take him
to the top of the mountain. Bind him.
Ready him for sacrifice to your God."

Rested, reassured Abraham awoke
the next morning. He had heard God.
He was ready. Surely Isaac would fight
so he would not be bound. Then Isaac
would awaken from his stupor
to become a man

in the eyes of Abraham
in the eyes of God.

Abraham told Isaac to accompany him
to the mountain to prepare a holy sacrifice.
Sarah watched anxiously as her husband and boy-man
wandered into the distant desert
becoming small against the horizon.
A cool breeze made her shiver.
Her body shuddered. She wanted to rush
out, urgently calling
her men back to her.

She could not let them go.
She must let them go.

Ascension

There was silence as father and son
walked in the desert. Isaac did not
question their destination.
Up the mountain they journeyed slowly
side by side.

Abraham told his servants to wait.
Only he and Isaac
ascended the mountain
alone
together.
Trusting but unsure
Isaac was happy to be alone
together with his father.
They walked slowly, Abraham trusting
God's voice inside him.

Bound, Unbound

Abraham announced they had reached
the place of sacrifice.
Isaac asked, "Where is the ram
for our sacrifice, father?"
Abraham did not answer as quietly
he began to bind his son
like an animal.

Helpless and suddenly alone
fear did not consume Isaac like a flame.
Isaac felt a presence even greater
than his father in this place.
He was filled with light
but it was not the light of fire.
A brilliant radiance filled him.

Like a distant dream
Isaac heard a voice ask
"Abraham, where are you?"
His father answered,
"Hineni, I am here"
and suddenly Isaac was free.
God was in this place
inside Isaac
surrounding him
on this mountain.
Isaac bathed in the light of God
until it blinded him.
Isaac was no longer bound
by the cords of Abraham.

The Sacrifice

A ram was stuck in a bush.
Isaac, no longer bound,
lovingly pulled the ram
out. He and his father
did not speak

as together they bound
the animal that did not cry out.
All was silent
on the mountain
as their sacrifice was made.

Abraham saw future generations
in the flames of the sacrifice.

Isaac only saw the flames of God's
Commandments.
Isaac took the ram's horn
to remember the animal sacrifice.
He used its horn in future years
to call his people together.

Coming Down

Father and son silent
descended the mountain.
Father and son alone
came down the mountain.
They did not hold hands.
Isaac did not need his father's hand
to guide him home. He was free
no longer bound
by his father's vision of him.

Change

Sarah anxiously waited and watched
for Abraham and Isaac. There was a blaze
of light in the distance coming closer.
Sarah was startled. Isaac was surrounded
by a glow of light. He was alone.
Abraham was not with him.

Isaac walked past Sarah
as if he did not see her.
Sarah's life drained from her being.

Isaac was safe.

Isaac wandered far into the fields
everyday. He always returned unharmed.
He no longer needed Sarah's
protection.

Sarah could no longer see
into Isaac's heart.
Sarah's heart wept for Isaac.
Her hope was lost.
Her faith betrayed.
She did not understand what happened
on the mountain.

Sarah watched Isaac from a distance.
Bathed in a glow of light, Isaac was
breathing wordless prayers.

Prayer in the Desert

For days, a hot desert silence
filled the tent of Abraham.
No words spoken.

Slowly building like a hum
a discordant mumbling, moaning
slowly, gradually ascending into
harmony of voices
joined and disjoined
all saying different words.
One continuous anguished stream of words
reaching.

Isaac and Sarah were
praying in the desert.
Together, separately
praying
that no more sacrifices
need be made.

Lot's wife

The Woman with No Name: Lot's Wife

And the angels warned Lot and his wife: "Do not turn around. Do not look upon the destruction." (Genesis 19:17)

Lot's path is straight.
Lot knows where to go.
Lot is good at leaving.
Lot runs ahead.

Lot's wife has carried her past
many times to new places. Like a heavy sack
upon her back it has grown heavier
each time she leaves. The sack has torn
open her heart leaving a trail of friends
and family she will never see again.
There is too much leaving.

Lot does not wait for her.
He shouts into the wind
"Do not look behind you. Do not gaze
upon the destruction." He keeps on going
ahead. His words echo inside her
pound like a drum against
her chest.

Blinded to the future
mourning the past, Lot's wife
stumbles, her vision
blurred by her sobs,
blurred by smoke from burning villages.
Heat, fire clouds her eyes. She cries
for mothers, babies, her daughters
whose screams fill the air
fill her ears as
smoke fills her nostrils.

Lot's wife stumbles on tears
turning to salt beneath her.

36

Heat from the fire of dying cities
drying the water of her eyes.
She cannot see where she is or
where she is going. Screams fill her.
She does not mean to disobey.
Her body twists to look behind.

She turns
into a pillar of salt
frozen in time.
She turns
into a pillar of remembrance
nameless like the people
of Sodom and Gomorrah.

Salt water tears
could not put out the fire
behind her.

Rebekah at the Well

"...behold, Rebekah came forth with the pitcher on her shoulder; and she
went down to the well and drew." (Genesis 24:45)

Rebekah carried her jug to the well.
She was graceful as a gazelle
strong as a camel. Her light dress
whispered warmly around her limbs
in the dry winds. Rebekah walked
to the well lost in thought
thinking of a dream she had that morning
in which an angel came to her and said,
"Go with the stranger."

A mysterious breeze caressed her shoulder.
She turned. No one was there but she
heard a voice tell her, "Go with the stranger."

She reached the well becoming lost in the
rhythmic motion of pulling the heavy
cord holding her bucket. Looking into the well
a vision of the future unfolded before her.

She did not see the stranger approach.
"Please let me sip a little water from your jar."
Rebekah without hesitation replied, "Drink,
my lord. I will also draw water
for your camels until they finish drinking,"
and she drew for all his camels.

Silently the man appraised her,
bowing homage to the God
of his master, Abraham, for guiding
him to this woman. He knew he had found
a wife for Isaac. His mission to his master
was fulfilled.

The Children of Rebekah's Womb

The children struggled in Rebekah's womb
and she said, "If so why do I exist?"
She went to inquire of the Lord
and the Lord answered her,
"Two nations are in your womb.
Two separate people shall issue from your body;
One people shall be mightier than the other,
And the older shall serve the younger."
(Genesis 25:22, 23)

Rebekah looked with wonder and fear
at the growing babies inside her
pushing under her skin.
She gazed with awe to see
an elbow or knee protruding outward.

Rebekah feared for her babies.
Rebekah feared for herself.
Her skin was pulled taut around her.
Her body pressed against itself
as if stretched to its limits.
Rebekkah cried out in the night,
"This is my greatest pain
This is my greatest joy!"
And Rebekah prayed:
"Let them be well, God.
Let me be well to know them."

The two nations expanded steadily
inside her womb. One moved
like a running animal, never still.
The other moved soft and gently
like a song on the lyre.

Rebekah looked down and watched them
roll atop one another,
push each other, vie for space.

Rebekah felt the quickly-moving one
bray like a confined animal banging
against her insides. Rebekah favored
the restful one who moved gently inside her.

Rebekah's twins

Birth of Rebekah's Twins

"The first came out red, his body a hairy mantle; so they named him Esau.
His brother came out gripping Esau's heel; so he was named Jacob."
(Genesis 25:25, 26)

In the last days of her pregnancy
the children jostled each other
for position
to travel toward their destiny.

The first bounced his way into life.
Red, hairy and quick, he greeted the world
with a fiery cry. They named him Esau
meaning "red."

The second child longing to enter
the world caught his brother's
heel. He was pulled into the world
one step behind Esau.
They named the second son Jacob
meaning "heel."

Esau became an impulsive
strong hunter.
Jacob became a thinker,
a steady herder.

Esau was favored by his father
who had a taste for game. Hunter
Esau brought his father stews and meats.
Isaac envied his son's strength and
lack of fear.

Jacob was favored by his mother
who loved his gentle, steady ways.
Rebekah favored Jacob
because he was so much
like her husband, Isaac.

Rebekah Remembers God's Promise

"The older child shall serve the younger." (Genesis 25:23)

Jacob and Esau born minutes apart
torn apart
by differences in character.
Torn apart by
the promise of a blessing to be
bestowed upon the eldest child.

Jacob's mother remembered God's promise.
She believed the blessing of the father
belonged to the son who would lead his people.

She helped Jacob deceive his father
to receive the blessing.
Jacob's life's journey
was filled with deception
to his father
to his brother.
Jacob was deceived
by his uncle
by his own sons.
Deception through the generations.

But Jacob's wives gave birth
to the nations of Israel.
God's promise was fulfilled.

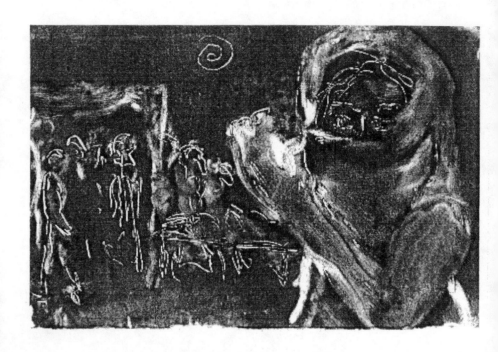

Leah before the wedding

Leah Speaks

Leah's Devotion

Simple, quiet
is the man who came to us.
He creates abundance
in the pasture.

I too am simple, quiet
I love him.
I believe he will come to love me
though I am short-sighted.

I know my sister, Rachel wants him
but she is beautiful, precocious
and favored by our father.
Surely there will be another for her.
She is so young.

A Steady Worker

The man, Jacob is a steady worker
He works here seven years.
I allow my father to deceive him
so I, the oldest will be married
before my younger sister marries.
I think he will come to love me.
I too am a steady worker.
I am devoted
full of love for this man
Jacob.

Deception

Sorrow of my soul!
My father has deceived me.
Rachel has also been promised
to my husband, Jacob.
My father used me

so that Jacob will stay on the land
to create abundance in
my father's fields and make the
animals flourish.

Jacob is blessed
but my life is sorrow.
Jacob is blinded.
He does not see
I love him.

We could be blessed together.

<u>Longing for love</u>

I was not my father's favorite child
and now my husband denies me love.
Love cannot be forced.
It cannot be bartered or traded.

How will he come to love me
when he waits for my sister?

Sorrow of my heart!
I have been deceived
yet there are moments in the darkness
when I think he cares for me.
His passion is a fountain
that bursts inside of me.
There is a spark of life between us
like that first night in the dark.

Surely his love blossoms
inside me.
If it is a boy
I will name him Reuben
for the Lord has looked upon me
and found favor within me.

Leah

Each son that I have born
from the womb of my love for Jacob
does not soften Jacob's heart.
It is not the total richness of his love
I desire. It is his blessing
I yearn for, to be whole
in his household
to raise our sons
amidst the blessings of the land
to share our joys and achievements
to live quietly and peacefully
on the land
with my husband.

Leah's Cry to Jacob

Our loving is quiet
a passive familiarity
but after loving
he is a man torn apart
unforgiving, bitter.
That is when I want to hold him
want to hold on, want him
to hold me
a bit longer.

I See You

I see your inner being.
Our children form in
quiet moments in the dark
when we do not need to see
just feel.
Moments in the dark
belong to only us.

In this darkness, Jacob
bring light.

For me, I ask nothing
but bless our sons.
Oh, Jacob, bless our sons.

Rachel Speaks

Beginning

Our eyes meet at the well.
We seek each other
and reach inside
down deep
pull the cool, refreshing waters
up to quench
the thirst of our souls.

Our love is immediate
blossoming
like a delicate, desert flower
too beautiful to pick.

Loving glances.
Tongues about to speak.
Two hearts hearing tunes from heaven.

Our young love is an open blossom
reaching toward the sun
outstretched arms waiting
with longing
to be filled.

Blossom

Seven years we wait.
My Jacob tends the sheep
and the flocks flourish.
Father is pleased.
The field of my future
looks bright with the promise
of many flowers.

The Blossom Begins to Fade

The blossom fades
in the dark
of what is to be my wedding night.
My father and sister deceive me.
Jacob lay with my sister in the dark.
He belongs to my sister now.
They are husband and wife.

Jacob is angered when he realizes
Leah is not me.
My father is afraid Jacob's anger
will affect the care of his flock.
It is me that Jacob loves.

My father again pledges me
to my lover in return
for seven more years of service
by Jacob to my father.
I am again pledged
to my lover. We must wait seven days.

We hold the promise of fulfillment
but I am not patient.
Seven days seems an eternity.
We have waited so long.
Jacob I want you now.

Wilted Flower

Blossoms shrivel
without water
without the fragrance of youth
and desire.

Jacob and I belong to each other
but the blessing that should have
been bestowed upon us alone is gone.

Traded like some magnificent jewel
for my lover's labor in father's fields,
anticipation and longing have
turned to loneliness and shame.
My status as leading woman
of the household is lost.
I am jealous of my sister
angry at Jacob, the one
I have longed to love.

I am empty
waiting to be filled.
We have only the memory
of the love we once sought.

Older Now

Leah grows ripe and proud
with Jacob's seed.

How can I not turn away
hide my shame, my envy?
If only it was me
full with Jacob's loving.

Jacob sees my hurt
yet he consoles me not.
Jacob sees my envy
yet he comforts me not.
Jacob sees my shame
and turns from me.

I am
empty
wanting
to be filled.

Open and Closed

He loves the one I was
not the one I have become.
His passion is foreign to me.
He is a stranger
I have loved from afar.

My Jacob,
Open me so I know you.
Close the wound that needs healing
after wanting you and waiting.

Close the wound and open me.
Jacob whom I love
Jacob whom I dream of
Jacob whom I share
with my sister Leah.

Longing

He makes fertile the ewes
so they multiply.
He makes fertile the womb of my sister.
His heirs are multiplied.

Their blessing is my curse.
My womb is empty.
Jacob whispers my name in the dark.
He holds me close.
Yet he will never be truly mine
until I give him an heir.

He whispers my name in the dark.
Yet it is Leah filled with his life seed.
She is soon to give birth
again.

My womb is empty.
"O God, give me children or I will die!"

The Mandrake

I traded a night of loving
for the mandrake found by
Leah's son.
The mandrake will make me fruitful.
The mandrake is my hope.
It holds the promise of fulfillment.

Blessing

Oh Lord of blessings.
I am with child!
Leah is with child!

Perhaps there will be
harmony in our home.
Our blessings are multiplied.

If it is a son, I will name him Joseph,
meaning "May the Lord give to me
another son."

Leaving

We have agreed to leave our home
and travel with Jacob to his home
far away. We leave this place
where I was born.

Can we leave the deception
of my father far behind?
I stole my father's idols,
his powers of strength.
Perhaps his idols will bring me luck?

Is my destiny to be fulfilled
on this journey
away
on this journey
home?

Rachel, Our Matriarch

Rachel, our matriarch,
is full of desire
passion and dreams.
She cherishes life.

Her love is as deep as the well
where she meets Jacob, her husband.
Her desire to become mother
to future generations
is ageless and without bounds.

She has a vision of the future-
for her children to love the land
for her children's children to flourish,
be mighty in their land
mighty in their love.

Once barren, like the land of Israel
she becomes fertile, celebrates life.
She knows the struggle
of wanting dreams to be fulfilled
knows the struggle
between passion and desire
disappointment and reality.

On her way to the promised land
Rachel, wife of Jacob, who becomes Israel
dies after giving birth
to Benjamin, her child of dreams.
She is buried on her way
to the promised land.

Buried along the road to Jerusalem
travelers hear her calling.
Rachel is calling her children to come to her.
Travelers hear her weeping. Sometimes they
hear laughter and joy. Sometimes
she is close to peace.

She comforts those in search of dreams.
Rachel knows desire
knows how dreams
may and may not be fulfilled.

Rachel, Mother of dreams
Mother to the children of Israel
across generations
we hear you calling.

A Traveler Hears Rachel Weeping on his Way to Jerusalem

(It is said that travelers can still hear Rachel weeping as they pass where she is buried.)

Hark! Who calls to me
in the middle of this road?
Is it Rachel weeping?
Does she grieve
because she lies alone?
Or is it Israel weeping
for her unborn children?

I am a traveler come
to make the land fertile
make the desert bloom
with lush, green richness.

O mother, Rachel, I hear your cry.
Your children will be born
here. I promise.

Rachel weeps

Handmaids to Rachel and Leah

"And Rachel said: 'Behold my maid Bilhah, go in unto her; that she may bear upon my knees' " (Genesis 30:3)
"When Leah saw that she had left off bearing, she took Zilpah her handmaid, and gave her to Jacob to wife." (Genesis 30:9)

<u>Bilhah Speaks</u>

We were the only property
our father owned. Sold
into slavery to Laban
father of Leah and Rachel.

I, Bilhah, handmaid to Rachel
bring her flowers of scintillating
scents to put in her long silky hair
that I love to comb. I make her sweet
smelling soaps for her delicate skin.
She is favored by her father for her
beauty. Rachel speaks softly to me,
accepts me though I am young.

My sister Zilpah, handmaid to Leah
guides Leah through her tasks.
Leah's soft blue eyes are weak.
She sees only Jacob clearly.
Leah wants Jacob.

Leah and Rachel treat us as their
sisters. They laugh with us
share their secrets, their sorrows.
We are blessed to be their maids.

Zilpah cannot bear her mistress' sadness.
Leah longs for Jacob,
has made herself sick

Now that Jacob is soon to
Marry Rachel. Zilpah plots with Laban
to let Jacob marry Leah first.
Leah is the oldest.
If both sisters marry Jacob,
Zilpah and I will remain together.

The Family of Jacob

Both our mistresses become wives
to Jacob. Leah is fruitful. She has
given Jacob several sons. Leah hopes
her heirs will make Jacob see her.
My mistress, Rachel longs for
children.

Our days are busy. Grinding wheat
is back-breaking work. I mix meal
with salt and water to bake bread everyday
in our mud-pit oven. Zilpah cuts and
gathers vegetables, dries meats to
mix with onions and garlic for stew.
We meet friends while doing laundry then
carry water from the well. We make
soaps and scented oils.
Our greatest game is treading grapes.
Squeezing juice from the fruit
tickles our toes, making us laugh.
We join family festivities
fuel the fires, fill oil lamps.

Bearing Bilhah

Rachel is barren. She has chosen to offer
me to Jacob in her name. I am
so young. I fear bearing a child.
Jacob is gentle, but not passionate.
He has eyes for Rachel only.

I lie with Jacob many times.

I am to give birth!.
Rachel is excited as I sit
upon her thighs and knees, her
arms wrapped around my swollen belly.
Our baby will slip from my womb,
sliding down through our
legs into life.

Rachel names our baby "Dan" because
God has heard her cry
and given her a son. I suckle
Dan from my breasts. Rachel rubs his body
in salt, swaddles him in warmth..
"I have prevailed," Naphtali, my
second son, is named by Rachel. I
have raised my status as secondary
wife by bearing sons. My sons belong
to the family of Rachel and Jacob.
Rachel loves her sons.

Our Sons

Zilpah longs to share the sisterhood
of women. She is only
a servant, never to marry.
We are overjoyed when Leah
ceases to bear children and asks
Zilpah to lie with Jacob. Joyfully,
Zilpah bears him two sons, Gad and Asher.

Our boys frolic and play in the fields
together. They are loved
by their mothers.

It is more than we hoped for-
to have sons who perpetuate the
family name and property, add
work power to the fields.
Sons are the living promise
from God that Jacob will father
great nations. Our sons bring
Jacob deep satisfaction. He teaches
our sons to hunt and tend the fields.

Zilpah and I earn honor by hard work.
Our daily tasks maintain
our Hebrew family.

We are handmaids in history.
Birth-givers of tribes.

Dinah Speaks

Hear the silence.
between the words.
Hear the voice pleading for love,
attention. Listen to your daughter.
Hear her story.
Do not let her vanish
Into history.

Dinah

Dinah Dishonored

"Shechem, son of Hamor the Hivite, prince of the region, saw her, seized her and lay with her by force." (Genesis 34:2)

I do not speak for myself.
My story exists in the silence
between words. The white purity
between the lines written. If you
read only words
you miss my story.

I am the last child born to
Leah and Jacob. I am not a male child.
My father does not look upon me.
My brothers do not include me.
My mother does not hear my cries.

Yearning to discover womanhood
I wander far from home
dressed in my simple tunic of
soft shades. I long for knowledge,
a place to fit in. Colorful
clothing of Canaanite women
entices me. The women sparkle
like jewels in the dazzling sun of
the marketplace. Their bracelets,
anklets, earrings, necklaces jingle-jangle
music in the market air. Canaanite women
command attention. They are not
invisible like me. I watch them,
trying to imitate their graceful
sensuous movements. A song
within myself calls me to dance.
My body quivers,
wakens my whole being.

Prince Shechem sees me.
He watches me dance.
Desire flames in his eyes. I see
admiration and longing.

Fluttering like a butterfly,
twirling like a top, I dance.
Shechem's desire excites me.
He dances with me, moving his hips and
shoulders. He pulls me toward him,
raising my veil, looking into
my eyes. He sees me and lusts
after me, lifting me into the air
like I am a tiny bird.

He carries me quickly
to a private street,
sets me on the ground
pushing himself on top of me.
He rips my clothing.

His sudden force frightens me.
Stunned, I scream. Dazed.
Sick at heart, I hate myself
hate my body,
unsure of who or what
I am.

After his force,
he speaks kindly to me.
He proclaims love. Is not love
meant to be gentle?
Confused, sickened,
I cannot return home.

Shechem commands me to come
with him to his father's palace.
He beseeches his father to keep me.

Hamor, Shechem's father,
proposes marriage between
Shechem and me, even offers my father
any price to secure me for Shechem.
I am an object to be bartered
traded as a thing defiled.
Father agrees to marriage on
condition of circumcision for all
men of Hamor's town. Surprisingly
Hamor agrees. My father's
wealth may be worthwhile
to Hamor someday.

No one asks me what I want.
No one asks me how I feel.
No one but Shechem sees me.

My brothers, Simeon and Levi,
are outraged. How dare a
male Canaanite defile them?

They slaughter
by sword
all the men in Shechem's town
while the town is weakened
by circumcision.
Drunk upon destruction
my brothers despoil the women,
steal sheep and cattle,
bring shame to Jacob's name.

My body is covered in the
blood of my brothers' destruction.
I starve myself
hating my existence.
I disappear
between the lines of the story.
Hear my voice in the silence....

Sequel to Genesis...
Miriam of Exodus

The tree of life

Miriam Weaves a Basket

Miriam and her mother
weave a basket of bulrushes.
Carefully pitch and mud fill
the basket to make it waterproof.
Miriam swaddles the baby Moses snugly
in cloth, cuddles him warmly then
sets him gently afloat the Nile
in the basket.

Miriam hides, waits, watches
the princess arrive
hears the princess laughing
as her handmaids fan her.

The basket floats directly to
the princess. She squeals with delight
wondering what present has come her way.
She lifts the baby Moses
like he is a new play thing
to give her joy.
The baby does not cry out.
He gazes into the princess' eyes.
Her heart is won. Moses is safe!

Swiftly, quietly on daring feet
Miriam runs home to her mother.
Miriam learns to shape the future.
She senses her destiny, her deep connection
to her brother and her people.
She convinces the princess to allow
her mother to become
wet nurse
to her own son.

Miriam knows Moses must one day
learn his identity
his beginning.
Moses should know that faith
saved him in the bulrushes.

The princess who came to love him
could have let him die.
Jewish sons died each day.
Jewish children became slaves.
Moses, child of hope was protected.

Miriam's faith flourishes
like a field of wildflowers.
Miriam knows that someday
she and Moses
will help their people
to be free.

Across the Red Sea

"And Miriam the prophetess, the sister of Aaron, took a timbrel in her hand; and all the women went out after her with timbrels and with dances. And Miriam sang unto them..." (Exodus 15:20)

Miriam's voice opens
and rises like the walls of water
in the Red Sea.
Like a beacon of light
Miriam's voice leads us
to the other side
away from Egypt
away from the life we have known.

And when we are safely across
the Red Sea, Miriam rejoices
calling on us to sing and dance
celebrate our safety.
We hug our loved ones
through tears of relief
tears of joy, floods of tears
and fear for our future.

And Miriam calls on us
to sing and dance
and celebrate freedom.
But God speaks to Miriam
admonishing, "Do not celebrate
while my people die."

The Egyptian soldiers are
perishing in the floods of water.
When we turn and look
we are awed by God's miracle to us.
The Red Sea has opened a path
letting us pass unharmed
while Egyptian soldiers die.

Miriam, Moses and Aaron
gather us to them like so many
sheep in a flock, leading us
hurriedly into the wilderness.

We begin our flight
without time to rejoice
not knowing what lay ahead
without time to celebrate
our freedom.

We journey away from oppressors
into the desert
a long, long journey
where we find strength
within ourselves and
faith with our God.

Miriam Sings

Miriam's voice
is smooth as satin
soft intensity
serene
pure as a dove
with white wings.
White wings
spread over the Jewish people
for protection.

Miriam's voice
like a dove
urges peace
urges trust.

Miriam
does not falter
does not hesitate.
Miriam sings sure.

Miriam is one.
One voice with
the Jewish people.

Miriam sings
a soothing song of
strength
that soars and carries
her people Israel
across the Red Sea.

In the Desert God Also Spoke to Miriam

When we, the Israelites
are impatient
fearful, angry
we yell at the heavens
"Did we leave Egypt to go hungry?
How far must we journey?
We are tired.
We are afraid."
Miriam reaches out to us
speaks softly, patiently,
"A tent is enough home.
Bread is enough food.
We are together.
God is with us."

Miriam is mother and
sister to us all.
And God speaks to Miriam
who is patient, strong.
She speaks gently to us
when we are hungry
or without hope.

Miriam soothes us
while Moses seeks God
for sustenance.
Restlessness, agitation, fear
are growing in our camp.
We are lost and wandering
seeking comfort
while Moses is busy seeking, searching
silent to his people.
One man cannot comfort us,
answer all our needs.

God also speaks to Miriam.
Miriam and Aaron together
decide they too will speak for God.
They want to assure us
that God is listening
God is near
but when Miriam presumes to speak for God
God casts her away with leprosy
away from us.
Our beloved Miriam.
We are confused.

Moses again our strong leader
prays to God to intervene
to let Miriam return.
Moses, our leader prays
and Miriam returns
after seven days.

She walks to us
neither defeated nor destroyed.
Her spirit and faith intact.
We gather around her.
Our precious Miriam.
We rejoice and
we gather together under
God.

Miriam's Well

Miriam's well is deep
deep as eternity.

Miriam's well has water
when the desert is scorched
and dry
when the Jewish people are thirsty.

Miriam's well is a gathering place
for women to cluster together for
conversation and nourishment.
Her well is a gathering place
for children to drink, to play
to bask in the light
of their mothers' eyes.

Miriam's well is full and deep.
When the Jewish people are empty
they reach down into the well
and pull the water up, up
to parched, dry lips.

Miriam's well is full
full of faith and
deep as eternity.

Affirmation of Our Stories

God created woman
in her own image
so like Eve we can
reach for opportunities
to keep growing
to move forward.

We move forward even as
we reach back in time
bringing forth knowledge
of centuries past
to the present.

We affirm what we believe
learning and growing as we
find wholeness in ourselves
our womanhood
our stories.
The ancient words of Torah
hold wisdom, poetry
rhythm, music and
remembrance.

We raise our collective
consciousness of women,
create a circle
from the beginning of time
to now so that we can share
what we know of life,
open ourselves to understanding.
Be born anew.

Explanation and Commentary about the Women of Genesis

LILITH (Genesis 1:27)

The name Lilith is not mentioned directly in the Torah. Her story may have evolved from ancient Babylonian literature where Lil was a goddess of strong powers. She appeared in ancient Rabbinic literature about 2,000 years ago. The midrashic story places Lilith as Adam's first wife because there seems to be two creation stories in the Torah. The first declares, "Male and female, God created them and blessed them." (Genesis 1:27) The second story however, says that Adam was put into a deep sleep and God pondered the problem of a mate for Adam. Thus Eve was born.

All was going well between Adam and Lilith until Adam demanded that Lilith be subordinate to him. Lilith, who like Adam, was just discovering the world, wanted independence to act freely. She became angry and flew away to the Red Sea. The crossing of the Red Sea later became a symbol for freedom when the Jewish people left Egypt.

Lilith has been demonized in folklore and literature for wanting equality and choosing to leave Adam. She is said to travel in darkness. She has been held responsible for luring men from their wives, harming babies, and putting curses on women.

I choose to believe that when Lilith left Adam, she did not know the full extent of her powers and possibilities. After all, she had just recently been born. That does not mean her powers were used for destruction.

Many civilizations still struggle with the questions: "Should a woman be now demonized for making choices other than the ones expected of her? How much control and responsibility are women now allowed for their own lives?" Hopefully, we have evolved to have more freedom of choice. Lilith made a choice. Freedom of choice is a blessing.

EVE (Genesis 2:18 - 4:2)

"And the Lord God said, 'It is not good that the man should be alone; I will make a help mate for him.'" (Genesis 2:18) God put Adam into a deep sleep while God pondered the possibility of a mate for Adam. Eve was created. Standard interpretations say Eve was created from Adam's rib but the actual Hebrew word "tsela" could also mean "side." Thus Eve was equal to Adam; his other side, so to speak.

Separation is an important theme in Genesis. In the beginning of Genesis, God separates light from darkness, sky from earth, day from night, waters from the land. So it follows that there might have been further separation of one creation into two separate persons.

Curiosity and desire seem to be part of woman's makeup. The fruit must have been extraordinary to capture Eve's attention. Western tradition has interpreted the fruit as forbidden, however, God did not tell this to Eve directly. Eve reaches and takes the fruit. Reaching is a sign of a child growing and developing. I believe God applauds Eve's curiosity by giving her the power to conceive life.

The sacred act of union by man and a woman gives them the ability to procreate. If they had stayed in the Garden of Eden, they may not have died. They may not have been able to create new life. In the Garden of Eden, yearning for wholeness was born as well as the ability to procreate. God tells Adam and Eve: "Therefore shall a man leave his father and his mother, and shall cleave unto his wife: and they shall be one flesh." (Genesis 2:24).

Eve's Hebrew name, Hava, comes from the root word for life. Eve is said to be the mother of all life. Surely, this is an honor.

MRS. NOAH (Genesis 6:12,13,18; 7:11; 8:13,15,16)

Noah's wife patiently stood by Noah while he built an ark. She accepted Noah's mission. She had faith in his beliefs. The building of the ark probably kept Noah away from his everyday tasks yet we do not read of her complaints. She raised her sons well. They all traveled on the ark together with the animals. Although the Bible says that Noah was a man righteous in his time, Mrs. Noah must also have been righteous to have been saved from the flood.

Noah's family traveled together on the ark to safety. What a journey it must have been with all those animals! I'm sure Mrs. Noah and her sons and daughter-in-laws, had quite a lot of work to do caring for all those animals.

The Eve and Adam story is about our creation. The Noah story is a re-creation story. God makes a covenant with humankind. It is a new beginning.

SARAH (Genesis 11:29 - 12:20; 16:1 - 18:15; 20:1 - 21:13)

Sarah was Abraham's wife. Abraham had destroyed his father's idols and chose to believe in one God. Together, Abraham and Sarah left their home with Abraham's nephew, Lot. It must have been difficult for Sarah to leave the land of her family, but I believe she and Abraham shared a vision for their future.

God promises Abraham a son to carry on the covenant between Abraham and his descendants. Sarah desired a child for herself. She hoped to keep the covenant with God, yet she remained barren. When angels came to the tent of Abraham, Sarah was an old woman. The angels were disguised as weary travelers. They told Abraham that Sarah would bear a child. Sarah laughed. It is not clear from the Biblical text whether she laughed aloud or to herself. She was not near the travelers, but they knew she laughed. We are left to wonder how the travelers knew she laughed. Perhaps, Sarah knows they are messengers of God because they speak of her inner laughter.

Sarah names her son Isaac. The name means "laughter." This demonstrates that Sarah was not embarrassed by her laughter. Indeed, she seems proud of her laughter and proud that God should bestow this joy upon her in her old age.

Sarah adores Isaac, protects him and loves him unconditionally. The most legendary scene in Genesis is the binding (the Akedah in Hebrew) of Isaac. Was God testing Abraham or was Abraham testing God? Was it all a dream? Did Sarah know that Abraham was taking her beloved son to the

80

mountain to be bound as an animal like a sacrifice?

We rarely see Abraham in doubt. Abraham must sacrifice his control of the future to the leadership of his son. He has doubts about Isaac's skills to lead the people. Isaac is not aggressive or strong. Abraham must transfer his doubt to his faith in God to help Isaac lead. Abraham's doubts probably put a strain on the family relationships.

The binding of Isaac is about trust, sacrifice and surrender. After the binding of Isaac, the family interactions are surely changed forever.

HAGAR (Genesis 21:9-17; 25:12)

Sarah felt she was mother to the people who chose to follow Abraham and worship one God. However, when Sarah's womb remained barren, she feared that God's prophecy (that Abraham would father a great people) might not be fulfilled.

After ten years in the land of Canaan without getting pregnant, Sarah chose her maidservant, the Egyptian, Hagar, to bear Abraham's child. The law allowed Sarah to then claim the child as her own. After Hagar conceived, she became boastful and proud. There is animosity between the women. Ishmael, Hagar's son, becomes boastful and proud like his mother. He receives a lot of attention from Abraham, and his birth mother. Ishmael is headstrong and aggressive.

When Sarah eventually has a child, Ishmael's position in the household is challenged. Ishmael is probably unkind to the infant. Hagar and her son are sent away at Sarah's command. They are sent into the wilderness without food or water. When Hagar cries out to God, God provides a well and promises that Ishmael will be leader of a great nation.

LOT'S WIFE (Genesis 19:17)

Lot's wife has no name but we know her story. She turned to salt leaving Sodom and Gomorrah. She turned to look back upon the town being destroyed after having been warned not to look behind.

The interpretation that Lot's wife disobeyed, therefore she was turned to salt, is too simplistic. There is more to the story. Two of Lot's wife's daughters were left behind. Isn't it natural to turn to look behind if you hear moaning or people crying out in pain?

We often speak of a respected community person as a pillar of the community. A pillar is considered a monument of strength. The Torah uses the word "pillar" and not a hill or pile of salt.

Salt was a precious commodity in Biblical times. It kept meat fresh. It was needed in the hot desert. Babies were bathed in salt after birth. Salt is part of the ocean, which is timeless. Our tears contain salt. Perhaps, Lot's wife turned to salt because of her sorrow. We would not remember the towns of Sodom and Gomorrah except for the pillar of salt left in remembrance.

Near the shores of the Dead Sea, there are large observable salt forms. Are they a reminder of Sodom and Gomorrah?

REBEKAH (Genesis 24:15-67; 25:19 - 26:12; 27:1-46)

Rebekah is one of my favorite women in the Bible. When we first meet her at the well, we learn that not only is she physically strong, but she is strong-willed and kind. She draws water for the stranger and all his camels even though she does not yet know the stranger. The stranger is the servant of Abraham sent to find a wife for Isaac. When the stranger appraises her, he finds her graceful, beautiful and good-natured.

Rebekah accepts her destiny, traveling far from family and friends to be with Isaac. God speaks to her directly when she inquires of God. She has a vision for the future and does what she needs to do to fulfill the covenant with God. Even if it means asking her son to deceive her husband to receive his blessing. She seems to know Isaac's weaknesses, yet loves him nonetheless. She knows he favors Esau but does not chastise him. She just makes sure that the covenant with God is fulfilled.

LEAH (Genesis 29:16-30; 30:1-20)

Leah is the older daughter of Laban. Laban is a selfish man who favors his daughter Rachel. He knows that Leah loves Jacob and so does Rachel. He tricks Jacob on what is to be Jacob's wedding night to Rachel by substituting Leah. Leah's face is covered. Perhaps, Jacob is under the influence of wine from the wedding feast. He is deceived. Leah is now his wife. He has slept with her. Although Leah is said to have weak eyes, Jacob's eyes must have been inadequate for him to have been so easily deceived!

When Jacob complains to Laban, Laban plays on Jacob's guilt. He exclaims that Jacob deceived his own father by pretending to be his brother. Who is Jacob to complain? Laban claims that the oldest must be married first. Now that Leah is married, Jacob may also have Rachel as his bride.

We do not know if Rachel was privy to this deception. Perhaps knowing that Jacob adored her, she agreed to the deception because Laban told her that Leah must be married first. How difficult for two sisters to be married to the same man!

Leah and Jacob seem to have more in common than Rachel and Jacob. Leah and Jacob seem to be consistent, steady people and are not risk takers. They are both gentle, simple people.

Rachel seems to be more passionate. She has a sense of destiny that Leah and Jacob do not feel even after Jacob has a vision of the angels ascending and descending the ladder.

After Rachel's death, Leah and Jacob were probably more in tune with each other and needed to depend on each other more. They were buried together in the ancestral tomb at Machpelah. I believe they came to have deep affection and love for one another and that Leah found contentment.

RACHEL (Genesis 29:4-30; 31:1-55; 35:16-20)

Jacob falls in love with Rachel the first time his eyes meet hers at the well. Rachel is beautiful and graceful. She is the favorite daughter of her father. I have a sense that things come easily to Rachel.

Jacob works on Rachel's father's land. Laban, Rachel's father, asks Jacob what he should pay Jacob in return for his work in Laban's fields. Jacob responds that he will work seven years in return for Rachel's hand in marriage.

Rachel yearns for Jacob and to become head of his household. She is deceived by her father who substitutes her older sister Leah on what is supposed to be Rachel's wedding night.

It is unclear whether Rachel knows of this deception in advance. There is no record of her protesting. Perhaps, Laban has also deceived her.

Rachel is again promised to Jacob. She is confident that Jacob loves her so much that she will be head of the household. However, there is some kind of bond between her sister and Jacob. Leah becomes pregnant easily and bears four sons in a row. Rachel yearns to have a child and secure her position in the household but she remains barren. She is envious of her sister.

Rachel pleads with Jacob, "Give me children or I shall die." (Genesis 30:1) Jacob loves her but cannot provide the magic that will make her pregnant. Perhaps Jacob feels his love should be enough. Rachel feels unfulfilled. It seems that Rachel needs more than his love.

God opens Rachel's womb (Genesis 30:22-24) and she gives birth to Joseph. How happy Jacob must have felt to finally provide Rachel with her heart's desire. Jacob's name means "the Lord shall add to me another son." So with Joseph's birth Rachel is already yearning for another child.

Rachel dies in childbirth on the road to Bethlehem. She names her second son Benoni meaning "son of my sorrow" but Jacob changes his name to Benjamin meaning "son of my right hand." Joseph and Benjamin are greatly loved by their father.

BILHAH (Genesis 29:29; 30:3-7; 35:22,25; 37:2)

Bilhah is the handmaid given to Rachel by her father Laban when Rachel marries Jacob. As Rachel remained childless after several years, while her sister Leah had four sons, Rachel decided to give her handmaid to Jacob as a secondary wife to bear him children.

Bilhah gave birth to two sons, Dan and Naphtali. As was custom at that time, the boys were integrated into the family structure. They became two of the twelve tribes of Israel. Samson became a descendent of Dan and Naphtali's tribe was very large.

ZILPAH (Genesis 29:24; 30:9-10; 35:26; 37:2; 46:18)

Zilpah is the handmaid given to Leah when she became Jacob's wife. When Leah temporarily ceased to bear children, she followed Rachel's example and gave Zilpah to Jacob as a secondary wife.

Zilpah bore Jacob two children. As was the custom, Leah named the children. When the first son was born, Leah named him Gad, and the second was named Asher. They became two of the twelve tribes of Israel.

DINAH (Genesis 30:21; 34:1,3,5,13,25,26; 46:25)

Dinah is not a Biblical character that is mentioned very often. Perhaps, it is because many people like myself feel conflicted about her story. Her name is mentioned at her birth and then when she is raped. Usually people speak of the "Rape of Dinah." How sad that it is the most significant event of her life.

Dinah roams away from home and visits nearby Shechem. Prince Shechem lusts after her. He "took her, lay with her and defiled her." (Genesis 34:2) Although he takes her by force, he proclaims his love for her. Shechem's father, Hamor, offers Dinah's father any price he desires to secure Dinah for his son in marriage. So much does he want her that he agrees to Jacob's demand that all the men of his town be circumcised.

We do not hear what happens to Dinah after that. We hear that her brothers, Simeon and Levi, slaughter the men of the town of Shechem. Although their father Jacob is upset by what they do, he does not stop them. Jacob curses them at the end of his life. On his deathbed, when Jacob calls all his children to him, he does not mention his daughter.

MIRIAM (Exodus 2:1-9; 15:20-21; Numbers 3:3-13)

Although the stories about Miriam take place in Exodus, I chose to add poems about her because in many ways the story of the Exodus is another Genesis story. It is a story of rebirth. The Jewish people leave slavery, travel through the wilderness, and choose a new way of life. While traveling, they redefine who they are and what they believe. They are chosen by God to receive the laws of the Ten Commandments.

It is Miriam who is pivotal in this Genesis. She saves Moses by putting him in the bulrushes in a basket, then ensuring his safety. She has a vision of the future and makes sure Moses will know his true identity by convincing the princess that Miriam's mother should be Moses' nursemaid.

Miriam organizes and helps rally the people around Moses, possibly even convincing Moses of his destiny. She is identified as a prophetess. After the Jewish people cross the Red Sea, Miriam leads them in song and praise of God. The Song of Moses and Miriam in the Torah is a beautiful poem that may have been written by Miriam.

In the wilderness, Miriam provides comfort and care. I have a sense that Miriam relates to the people in a way that Moses cannot. She convinces the women not to give their jewelry to make the golden calf. In the desert, God provides "Miriam's well" that remains full of water.

Books about Genesis and Women of the Bible

Armstrong, Karen. *A History of God: The 4000-Year Quest of Judaism, Christianity and Islam.* New York: Alfred A. Knopf, 1993.

_____. *In the Beginning: A New Interpretation of Genesis.* New York: Alfred A. Knopf, 1996.

Bach, Alice and J. Cheryl Exum. *Miriam's Well: Stories About Women in the Bible.* New York: Delacorte Press, 1991.

Buchmann, Christina and Celina Spiegal, eds. *Out of the Garden: Women Writer's on the Bible.* New York: Fawcett Books, 1994.

Deen, Edith. *All of the Women of the Bible.* San Francisco: HarperCollins, 1983.

Frankel, Ellen. *The Five Books of Miriam: A Women's Commentary on the Torah.* New York: G.P. Putnam's, 1996.

Heaton, E.W. *Everyday Life in Old Testament Times.* New York: Charles Scribner's Sons, 1956.

Lockyer, Herbert. *All the Women of the Bible: The Life and Times of All the Women of the Bible.* Grand Rapids, MI: Zondervan Publishing House, 1988.

Meehan, Bridget Mary. *Praying with Women of the Bible.* Missouri: Liguori/Triumph, 1998.

Moyers, Bill. *Genesis: A Living Conversation.* New York: Doubleday, 1996.

Rosenblatt, Naomi and Joshua Horwitz. *Wrestling With Angels: What Genesis Teaches Us About Our Spiritual Identity, Sexuality and Personal Relationships.* New York: Delacorte, 1996.

Steinsaltz, Adin. *Biblical Images.* New York: Basic Books, 1984.

Twain, Mark. *The Diaries of Adam and Eve.* Canada: McGraw Hill, 1971.

Visotzky, Burton L. *The Genesis of Ethics.* New York: Crown Publishers, Inc., 1996.

Zornberg, Avivah Gottlieb. *Genesis: The Beginning of Desire.* Philadelphia: Jewish Publication Society, 1995.

About the Artists

Sherri Waas Shunfenthal is a Northern Virginia free-lance writer/poet whose poetry has appeared in magazines, books and on artwork. Her most recent poetry appears in *Family Celebrations* (Andrew McMeel Publishers) and Fodderwing Magazine. Her essay, "Pauses" appears in *Every Woman Has a Story* (Warner Books Publishers).

Sherri has an M.S degree in speech/language pathology. She has combined her love of language, people, and poetry to form Poetry Partners, interactive poetry workshops for ages 2 to 90. Poetry is a partnership between the listener, reader, writer and the words.

Sherri has also written prayers and poems for special occasions. She wrote the Yom Kippur Children's prayer service for Adat Reyim Synagogue. Sherri hopes to fill the whole world with poetry. She can be reached at Sherrifern@erols.com.

Judybeth Greene is an attorney and an artist whose works on Judaic and secular themes have appeared in local venues from Eastern Market in Washington, D.C. and galleries to Fabrangen's high holiday services. Boston-born, Judybeth began her artistic career at age thirteen, selling macrame wall hangings in New England crafts fairs; in her late teens, Judybeth sold macrame haircombs in local Boston boutiques such as Fiorucci's in Haymarket Square. Her newer works display her growth as a printmaker and painter.

The lyrical artwork Judybeth designed to accompany this book was specifically inspired by Sherri's intimate and beautiful use of words. The genesis of Judybeth's current work is her love of texture and movement and her celebration of the human spirit. Whether a piece features her "flying figures" or dancers, or focuses on Judaic or spiritual issues, the message that emerges generally relates to a person's inner core and to connectedness, with oneself, with others, or with a higher being.

Judybeth developed as an artist through her own course of study, taking Intensive workshops across the country as well as classes at local schools such as the Washington Studio School and the Corcoran. She experiences the process as magic and spiritual one, stating that her "greatest joy is seeing people connect with my art on a heart-felt level."

To find out more about the artist, Judybeth can be reached via email at:

JudybethG@aol.com or at P.O. Box 33315, Washington, D.C. 20033-0315.

Pocol Press "Your Hometown Publisher"

6023 Pocol Drive, Clifton, Virginia 20124-1333
Tel: (703) 830-5862
E-mail: chrisandtom@erols.com
FAX: (603) 215-3557
http://members.xoom.com/Vonderahe/pocolpress.htm

Pocol Press seeks new stories/manuscripts in nearly every genre. We're perfect for first-time, unagented authors, but, all submissions welcome. Pocol Press is NOT a vanity press and does not ask for money from authors to publish their works of art.

Sacred Voices: Women of Genesis Speak by Sherri Waas Shunfenthal. Illustrations by Judybeth Greene, Pocol Press, 100 pp., 2000, $13.95. The Biblical women of Genesis awaken to tell their own stories in lyrical poetry. Begin to understand the thoughts, feelings and motivations of these women. Hear the voices of Eve, Mrs. Noah, Lot's wife, Rebekah, Rachel and others speaking to you as if they are friends confiding their innermost thoughts. ISBN: 1-929763-07-7.

MISFITS! Baseball's Worst Ever Team by J. Thomas Hetrick, Pocol Press, 216 pp., 1999, $17.95. The tragicomic story of the hapless 1899 Cleveland Spiders, baseball's futility leaders and winners of but 20 out of 154 games that year. Meet some of the most colorful characters ever to wear major league uniforms. Follow their hysterical train-travel odyssey through the National League and straight into historical obscurity. So pathetic were these Spiders that on the season's final day, a cigar store clerk became their starting pitcher. Wondrous anecdotes abound. Reviewed in *1999 Cleveland Indians Yearbook*. Illustrations, appendices, sordid statistics, bibliography, and index. ISBN: 1-929763-00-X.

Unusual Circumstances, various authors, compiled and edited by J. Thomas Hetrick, Pocol Press, 150 pp., 1999, $13.95. "If you had one hour to do anything you wanted, what would you do?" Such is the premise from author Sue Fuerst in her story *The Hour Glass*. The initial offering of quality fiction for the Short Story Anthology Project, this arresting collection explores the unlimited vagaries of the human condition. Examined are age-old issues of love and hatred, fear, loneliness, revenge, unbridled happiness, delusions of grandeur, depression, sexuality, and hope. Featuring the talents of Brian Ames, Jack De Vries, Paul Perry, H. H. Morris, Steven Riddle, and Jessica Slater. ISBN: 1-929763-03-4.

The Genealogy Anthology Project. Now accepting submissions for a book, this popular anthology highlights family stories of loved ones—ordinary people alive or long departed who have committed extraordinary acts. You've done the research. Now it's time to celebrate the lives of your loved ones or distant relatives.

Other books by the editor of this volume
Chris Von der Ahe and the St. Louis Browns by J. Thomas Hetrick, Scarecrow Press, 284 pp., 1999, $42.00. Biography of remarkable 19th century baseball owner and rapscallion. Illustrations, statistics, appendices, bibliography, index. ISBN: 0-8108-3473-1. www.scarecrowpress.com

TO ORDER:
Specify title and send personal check, money order, or cashier's check. Add $2.00 shipping and handling per book. Priority mail $4.00 S+H per book. Foreign orders extra. Payable to: Pocol Press.